The Scienti

Why science is a crucial **process** for human progress, not just another academic subject or belief.

Gordon Holman

Copyright © 2023 Gordon Dean Holman
All rights reserved
ISBN-13: 9798853953949

Cover photo credit: Casey Horner, silhouettes of trees under starry sky, 2018, Yosemite Valley

The Scientific Method in a Nutshell

Ask questions! Follow the steps below to seek an answer to one of these questions.

1. Start with a statement (**hypothesis**) to be tested that is based on your question.

   A valid scientific hypothesis

   - **cannot** be proven to be absolutely true
   - **can** possibly be shown to be incorrect.

2. Make a **prediction** based on the hypothesis.

3. Search for any information already available pertaining to the validity of the hypothesis and prediction.

4. Make **observations** or devise an **experiment** to test the prediction. Examine the results of the observations or experiment. The results should be

one thing if the hypothesis is acceptable, and something else if it is incorrect.

A hypothesis is acceptable and useful as long as it has not been demonstrated to be incorrect.

5. Revise or change the hypothesis if required by the results. When multiple valid hypotheses can be envisioned, **always choose the simplest hypothesis**.

6. Make methods and results public for comments and future studies. (If you are a professional scientist, **publish** in an appropriate refereed journal and present at scientific society meetings.)

7. **Repeat** with a new experiment or observations to test a refined or revised hypothesis.

Table of Contents

i. Title Page   i
ii. Copyright Page   ii
iii. The Scientific Method in a Nutshell   iii
iv. Table of Contents   v
v. Acknowledgments   vi
1. Why This Book?   1
2. Hypotheses, Laws, Theories, and Models   11
   Hypotheses and Predictions   11
   Laws   17
   Theories   18
   Models   21
3. The Scholarly Side of Science   23
4. Observations, Experiments, and Instrumentation   29
   Experimentation   30
   Observations   35
   Chapter Summary   46
5. The Importance of Simplicity   49
6. Science is a Group Activity   61
7. How Much Do You Believe a Hypothesis? Give me a Number!   67
8. Good Work! Now Do It Again.   81
   The Scientific Method in a Nutshell   88
   About the Author   91

Acknowledgments

I thank my wife, Barbara Holman, for proofreading the text and finding errors my mind could not see.

Chapter 1
Why This Book?

This book is for both the general public and scientists. My initial motivation for writing it came when I realized that, after having been a working scientist for several decades, I could not give a clear answer if asked the question "What is the Scientific Method?" So, as anyone with strong academic credentials and curiosity would do, I searched the internet. I found some information on the topic, but I did not find it to be particularly satisfying. What I found was to my mind either oversimplified and, therefore incomplete, or long-winded without converging on a clear, complete answer.

Next I decided to ask a few scientist colleagues to describe the Scientific Method to me. Their answers were basically along the lines of "test, retest, and test again". (I am oversimplifying here somewhat for brevity.) This answer is certainly relevant but even less satisfying than what I found on the internet. It does emphasize, however, the semi-repetitive aspect of the Scientific Method that is apparently not appreciated by many non-scientists.

It occurred to me that the Scientific Method is most likely to have been taught in introductory science courses. Since I majored in physics in college, I dug up my freshman physics textbook. Nothing.

My freshman chemistry textbook also had nothing. I looked at a number of science texts I had kept without any success. An old astronomy textbook by the astronomer George Abell did at least contain a mention of it[1]. He makes the important distinction between following the Scientific Method and inventing explanations out of one's imagination for explaining the nature of the Universe.

My internet search did reveal multiple tutorials with six- or seven-step ordered listings of the Scientific Method. These listings (similar but not identical) and the brief discussion associated with them are quite useful to secondary school students, their parents, and teachers who are motivated to search for them. As an example application of the Scientific Method, a couple of the sites[2] use the diagnosis of a broken electric toaster. This example has the nice feature that it illustrates the applicability of the Method to common household problems. I will return to it later in the book.

Although the logic of the Scientific Method is great for solving problems, more important is that it provides a guideline for making

---

[1] Abell, George, Exploration of the Universe, Brief Edition (Holt, Rinehart and Winston, Inc.), 1969.

[2] Khan Academy > Science > High school biology > Biology foundations > Biology and the scientific method (https://www.khanacademy.org/science/high-school-biology/hs-biology-foundations/hs-biology-and-the-scientific-method/a/the-science-of-biology);

Course Hero > Boundless Psychology > The Scientific Method (https://www.coursehero.com/study-guides/boundless-psychology/the-scientific-method/)

new discoveries about ourselves, our environment, and beyond. When applied thoughtfully and repeatedly, following it leads to a deeper understanding of an original discovery and to new, related discoveries. For scientists it also typically leads to more questions than answers. The many answers that have been obtained, however, have changed all of our lives, from longer, healthier lives to computer-based electronics and communications to knowledge of our Solar System and the Universe beyond.

To my surprise I have found the claim that there is no Scientific Method[3]. It doesn't exist! The argument is that scientists do not follow a formal method. Instead, science succeeds because of two ethical principles. The first is that scientists agree to always tell the truth, based on rational thinking and public evidence, and agree to be open minded to new evidence and ideas. The second is that scientists agree to encourage competition and diversification among professionals in the community.

Both of these principles are important to the success of science. A dishonest report of an experimental or observational result can substantially set back progress in an area of science. Ideally, an incorrect result will be identified by the repetition of testing inherent to the Scientific Method. The second ethical principle of competition and diversity increases the likelihood that any errors or dishonesty will be identified. If an area of science becomes relatively

---

[3] Smolin, Lee, There is No Scientific Method, bigthink.com, May 01, 2013. (https://bigthink.com/articles/there-is-no-scientific-method/)

inactive, however, incorrect results are more likely to become ingrained in the scientific literature.

As noted in the second paragraph of this chapter, many scientists cannot provide a clear description of the Scientific Method. They go about their work without explicitly thinking about it. With increased complexity as science progresses and greater numbers of scientists, they may primarily work on only one aspect of the Scientific Method, such as models, theories, or instruments for experiments or observations. Also, there is no single, accepted listing of the Scientific Method. So does this mean that the Scientific Method is irrelevant and scientists are solely motivated by these ethical considerations?

It is clear to me the answer is no. If the Scientific Method is repeatedly followed by a community of scientists, the results will be consistent with these ethical principles. The Scientific Method does not work without honesty, but it contains a mechanism for identifying dishonesty. It seeks consensus, but it does not ask you to believe anything, including the Scientific Method itself! Instead it is a prescription, based on centuries of experience, for obtaining reproducible information about yourself, your environment, and the Universe in general. It, not ethical principles, encapsulates what is unique about the sciences.

I am a retired scientist. Like many retired people, I spend more time listening to politicians than required to be a good, responsible citizen. I frequently hear politicians say that something is "just common sense". I often find that their common sense is not my idea of common sense. The term itself certainly contains no rational justification (It doesn't need one since, after all, it is common sense?) and one is seldom given. Therefore, I have concluded that "common sense" is just another form of "bandwagon" propaganda — "everyone believes it, so you should too". Information obtained through the Scientific Method is genuine "common sense". It is obtained through a rational, systematic approach, and a substantial number of other people have verified that they obtained the same results. However, "it is just common sense" would never be an acceptable answer to a scientific question.

I have heard or seen statements or signs saying something along the lines of "science is fake news". This statement is meaningless on several levels. At the fundamental level, I can't think of any information that less qualifies as "fake news" than news obtained with a full implementation of the Scientific Method.

So, what is the Scientific Method? I have provided a summary near the front (and back) of this book. As I stated earlier, there is no universally accepted listing of it, but all the listings at least contain the general concept. You can find it shown elsewhere as a block diagram[4], as one might produce to show the logic of a computer algorithm. For simplicity and alignment with the chapters of this book, I have decided to stick with a linear presentation. It has also been called the Experimental Method, but I have generalized it to include either experiments or observations. Some branches of science such as astronomy depend more on observations than

---

[4] Science Buddies > Science Fair Projects > Science Fair > Steps of the Scientific Method (https://www.sciencebuddies.org/science-fair-projects/science-fair/steps-of-the-scientific-method)

experiments. I have also generalized it to include important requirements for a hypothesis.

Unfortunately, even this expanded summary is not complete. There is no information about how to formulate a good hypothesis. There is also no information about how to design a good experiment or choose appropriate observations to test the hypothesis. Entire books can be and have been written about both of these subjects. Although the Scientific Method may looks like a dry list of instructions to some people, these are areas that allow for a great deal of creativity and, potentially, confusion. Even the words "acceptable" and "incorrect" need further discussion.

The purpose of this book is to provide a non-technical, practical presentation and discussion of the Scientific Method with examples for the general public. This is not a textbook or a philosophical treatise. There is no extensive discussion of historical and philosophical origins. The focus is on what it is and how it works with examples from both everyday life and the sciences. I have tried to avoid long diversions from the main points while keeping the discussion light, interesting, and easy to read.

I had not planned to write a book, especially one outside my specific field of specialization, given the current proliferation of books and online information. I find that for any thought I might have that seems interesting I can find something similar somewhere on the internet. I decided to write this after I could not find a book or Web site that focuses with some depth on the individual steps of the Scientific Method. For non-scientists, I hope this book will provide a better understanding of scientific thinking and what scientists do. For scientists, this book will hopefully sharpen some thoughts about the Scientific Method and how to explain it to others.

I have tried to keep this book general to all the sciences. My field of specialization is astrophysics, however, so the examples will have some bias toward this field.

The next chapter (Chapter 2) delves into the art of formulating a hypothesis. The value of a result obtained from application of the Scientific Method is only as good as the quality of the question asked and the corresponding hypothesis and prediction to be tested. This chapter also looks at laws, theories, and models and how they differ from hypotheses. There is considerable confusion in the general public about how these differ and the level of confidence scientists have in them.

Before carrying out observations or an experiment to test a hypothesis, it is important to learn what is already known about the topic. Prior knowledge can and should have a strong impact on how the hypothesis is chosen. The amount of information available on almost any scientific topic can be overwhelming, but search engines help to make up for this. The scholarly side of scientific research is discussed in Chapter 3.

Although all the steps of the Scientific Method are important for scientific research, the best known and most fundamental is experimentation and/or observations, typically with specialized instruments. The success of this step depends on an ability to obtain a clear test of the prediction. The instruments used must be capable of providing this test. Insufficient technology for producing the required instruments often slows progress in a scientific field.

Development of this technology often proves to be valuable in areas beyond this original investigation. On the other hand, instruments (and scientists) require money. In Chapter 4 I provide historical examples to illustrate these issues.

In the pursuit of an answer to a scientific question there is frequently more than one hypothesis that can be put forward. When you have multiple hypotheses, how do you choose? Do they all need to be tested? The answer is to always choose the simplest hypothesis. This step is not generally included in listings of the Scientific Method. In Chapter 5 I argue that it is critical and should always be included. I also discuss the question "What do you mean by 'simple'?"

Most scientific research today is complex enough that it is carried out by a group rather than an individual scientist. Individual scientists can and do make significant discoveries, but they do it as part of an institution that supports their work. They typically receive substantial support from sources outside their institution as well, such as national government. Obtaining this support is usually competitive, with panels of scientists reviewing proposals they write and submit. Likewise, scientific results are not generally accepted until they and the methodology for obtaining them are carefully described in a paper that is reviewed and commented on by at least one outside scientist and published in a scientific journal. Before the results are accepted in the scientific community, they need to be tested by others until general agreement is reached that they are valid. As discussed in Chapter 6, science is truly a group activity.

Since scientific hypotheses cannot be proved to be absolutely true, the most solid scientific results have been tested, used, and applied to such an extent that they are generally considered to be facts. Not all hypotheses can be this firmly established, however. Sometimes a hypothesis looks promising but cannot be established with high confidence, at least not yet. Sometimes more than one hypothesis look promising, but it is difficult to prefer one over the other. (The simplicity argument doesn't always work.) In these cases probability and statistical methods exist to attach a number to your confidence in a hypothesis. Chapter 7 discusses these methods and when it is likely be worthwhile to implement them.

Science is a never-ending process. If a hypothesis is determined to be incorrect, the Scientific Method says to start over with a new hypothesis. Finding a hypothesis to be incorrect is not a failure. It is acquired knowledge showing what is not an acceptable answer to a question and possibly indicating what new hypothesis should be tested. If a hypothesis is found to be acceptable, the Scientific Method says to continue testing it, preferably with a new experiment or observation and possibly another prediction, until a community of scientists can agree that it is acceptable. An acceptable hypothesis leads to more specific, more refined hypotheses and a new, deeper understanding of the topic being studied. Hence, more questions to be answered. This continuing process is discussed in Chapter 8.

In this book I use historical examples to illustrate the various aspects of the Scientific Method. Since this is not a book about the history of science, these examples are not individually referenced. They are well known and can be found with additional details and references online in Wikipedia and other encyclopedic works. I certainly recommend learning more about these and related examples online and at your local library.

Chapter 2
Hypotheses, Laws, Theories, and Models

Hypotheses and Predictions

Scientific studies start with a question. If you live in a region with lots of trees, at some point in your life you hopefully ask yourself the question "Why are all the trees green?" This question needs some refinement, however, because you quickly remember that they have limbs and a trunk that are mostly brown and the leaves are the green part. You also remember that the green leaves are gone or brown in the winter. Therefore, using this prior knowledge, a better question is "Why do all the trees have green leaves in the summer?"

The Scientific Method starts with a testable statement, a *hypothesis*, derived from your question. This question can be fully addressed with the following hypothesis: "All trees have green leaves in the summer because the leaves reflect green light and all other colors are absorbed by the leaves."

This hypothesis makes two separate *predictions*. The first is "All trees have green leaves in the summer." This prediction is in principle testable because you can observe trees in the summer and see if they have green leaves. From a practical point of view, however, you are unlikely to be able to observe all trees. Therefore, you decide you could look at all the trees in a nearby forest that is only a few acres in extent.

You might expand this hypothesis and corresponding prediction to include plants and grass, since you see that they are also green. To keep your hypothesis focused and manageable, however, you decide to limit it to trees. On the other hand, you know that ornamental trees around the neighborhood can come originally from all over the world, while trees in the forest are mostly native. Therefore you decide to add the neighborhood trees to your sample of trees to be observed.

So you go out in the summer and look at all the trees in your neighborhood and the nearby forested area. You find that all but two of the trees, both in your neighborhood, have green leaves. These two trees have reddish leaves. Therefore you conclude that your hypothesis is incorrect. You note, however, that most of the trees did have green leaves. If you counted a total of 100 trees, 98% had green leaves.

A scientific hypothesis can never be proved to be 100% true, which we refer to as absolutely true. Only statements in a man-made system of definitions and rules such as logic or mathematics can be shown to be absolutely true. If you place three coins on a table and state that three coins are on the table, your statement is absolutely true by definition. The statement "2 + 2 = 4" is absolutely true because it is based on the definitions and rules of mathematics.

In testing the "All trees have green leaves in the summer." prediction, it may seem that, if all the trees had been observed to have green leaves, the prediction would be absolutely true. It would be if the hypothesis included the location and date of the observations. The purpose of a scientific hypothesis, however, is to discover universal truths, not something that is true at a particular location or time only. A sample of trees from another location may have given a different result. A hypothesis or theory is often stated to be true. What this actually means is that the hypothesis has been so thoroughly tested that it is generally agreed to be true. Alternatively, it can be stated that there is 99.9999…% confidence in the validity of the hypothesis

While a scientific hypothesis is never 100% proven, it only took one tree to demonstrate that the "All trees have green leaves in the summer" prediction is incorrect. The failure of this prediction is not a bad result, however. It shows that the hypothesis should now be "98% of trees have green leaves in the summer because the leaves reflect green light and all other colors are absorbed by the leaves." There is no reason to have much confidence in the 98% number. Another sample of trees may give a different number. In fact, by observing many distinct samples of trees, this number will be refined and we can estimate how much confidence we should have in the refined number.

The second prediction from our hypothesis is "Trees have green leaves because the leaves reflect green light and all other colors are absorbed by the leaves." This part of the hypothesis and this corresponding prediction make use of some prior knowledge.

Although the hypothesis falls into the biological sciences category, this prior knowledge comes from the physical sciences. We know that light from our Sun that reaches the surface of the Earth contains all the colors of the visible spectrum and beyond. Therefore, if all of these colors were reflected by a leaf it would have the whitish color that results from the combination of all of these colors. Since the leaf looks green, predominantly green light must be reflected to our eyes. The other colors might be scattered away from our eyes, but the leaf looks green from all angles. Therefore the other colors must be absorbed by the leaf.

   One way this prediction can be tested is by shining different colored lights on a leaf. If the prediction is correct the leaf should be dark except when it is illuminated by a green light. A better way to carry out this test would be to use a spectroscope, an instrument that measures the intensity of the light reflected by the leaf across the visible spectrum. It may turn out that the other colors are not completely absorbed and the hypothesis will need some modification. It may turn out that the results are somewhat different for different leaves. Every modification or change that needs to be made to the hypothesis is scientific progress that leads to new knowledge and deeper questions.

   What if the part of the hypothesis corresponding to the second prediction had instead been "Trees have green leaves because God made them green." This is not a scientific hypothesis because it is not testable. There is no observation or experiment that can be done to test this hypothesis. Worse, it is a dead end to this line of enquiry.

The Scientific Method

Our scientific hypothesis, on the other hand, leads to more questions and an even deeper depth of understanding.

The discussion of this example shows that the nature and quality of a hypothesis substantially determines where a scientific enquiry leads. Testing the two predictions from this hypothesis provides some valuable results, but not an answer to the intent of the original question. We know that trees are living things. Testing this hypothesis revealed that most, but not all trees have green leaves. Therefore we conclude that whatever causes the leaves to reflect primarily green light must be important to keeping the trees alive. The question can now be written "Why is it important to the lives of most trees to have green leaves?" We also now have the additional questions "How can some trees stay alive with reddish leaves?" and "Why might it be advantageous for some trees to have reddish leaves?"

We know from physics that light carries energy. Therefore leaves absorb energy from the Sun. How does the leaf use that energy to maintain the life of the tree? Our next working hypothesis could be "Leaves contain a molecule that absorbs light energy but reflects green light." To make progress, we would need to separate the chemical components out of the leaf. The testing of this hypothesis is stalled until this capability is obtained.

The purpose of the above discussion is not to provide a tutorial on the interesting topic of plant biology. Rather it is to provide examples of scientific hypotheses and predictions. It shows how a simple question can lead to multiple hypotheses and predictions through application of the Scientific Method. Your knowledge and understanding increase and deepen with each tested prediction. Your questions and hypotheses also deepen and become more specific with increasing knowledge. The Scientific Method ensures that questions become specific enough to be tested and new knowledge comes from observations or experimentation.

Let's now return to the example of a broken electric toaster mentioned in the previous chapter. A hypothesis can help diagnose what is wrong with the toaster. Several hypotheses could be considered, depending on how much you know about electric toasters. It makes sense to first pose a hypothesis that is easily tested. This is most likely "The electrical receptacle the toaster is plugged into is broken." This can be tested by plugging another, working electrical device such as a lamp into the same receptacle. If the lamp works, the hypothesis is incorrect. If the lamp doesn't work, the receptacle is probably the problem.

If we were diagnosing a lamp instead of a toaster and the receptacle apparently works, the next hypothesis would probably be "The light bulb is burned out." The next step for the toaster depends on how knowledgeable or adventurous you are with electric toasters. In any case, the Scientific Method is useful for diagnosing problems. Would you have followed this line of thought if you were not familiar with the Scientific Method? Quite possibly. Much of the Scientific Method is what many people would call "common sense".

Is a statement such as "The electrical receptacle the toaster is plugged into is broken." a scientific hypothesis? It is a useful hypothesis, but it is not a scientific hypothesis because it does not address a universal feature of the natural world. Here *natural world* means anything in the Universe, including plants, animals and people, that is not made or caused by people.

In brief, a *scientific hypothesis* is a possible answer to a question about the natural world that can be tested by observations or experimentation.

Laws

A *scientific law* is a statement about the natural world based on observations or experiments that describes some aspect of the world. Scientific laws often describe a relationship between one observed quantity and another. Like hypotheses, laws cannot be proven. They describe phenomena and relationships, but typically do not explain them.

A simple example is Boyle's Law, established in the 17th century. It states that for a gas at constant temperature, reducing its volume increases its pressure. More specifically, pressure times volume is constant. This is a well-established relationship and, therefore, qualifies as a law rather than a hypothesis.

Another example is Newton's First Law of Motion. This states that an object will remain at rest or in uniform motion with constant speed along a straight line unless acted on by an external force. The statement that an object in uniform motion will remain in uniform motion is not obvious from everyday experience or simple experiments. If you push or throw a ball or any other object it eventually slows down and stops. It frequently does not follow a straight line.

This important law was established through the power of inductive reasoning. Let's treat Newton's First Law of Motion as a hypothesis and "An object in uniform motion remains in uniform motion." as a prediction from the hypothesis. If we throw a ball in a horizontal direction it always drops to the ground. If we push an object across a surface it always slows and stops, but at different distances depending on the object and the surface. An object pushed downhill goes farther than the same object pushed uphill with the same force. We never achieve uniform motion. The prediction is incorrect. When the final phrase, "unless acted on by an external force", is included, the hypothesis is acceptable.

The First Law tells us that we should be looking for one or more external forces on the object. On Earth these are typically gravity, friction, and drag from motion through the air. Although never-ending uniform motion is not achievable on Earth, the concept produces a simpler, more useful law.

Theories

A *scientific theory* is an explanation of some aspect of the natural world that has been tested and substantiated through repeated observations or experiments. While a hypothesis is a testable statement about the natural world, a theory is a well-tested hypothesis or a unified explanation for multiple well-tested hypotheses.

Like a hypothesis, a theory cannot be shown to be absolutely true. Many theories have been so thoroughly substantiated using the Scientific Method, however, that they are understood to be broadly

The Scientific Method

true. The kinetic theory of ideal gases, for example, provides an explanation for the observed properties of gases in terms of the random motions of the microscopic particles that make up the gas. It provides a natural explanation for Boyle's Law, discussed above.

A well-substantiated theory typically does have limitations. The kinetic theory of ideal gases assumes that all the microscopic particles that make up a gas are identical and there is no force or energy exchange between them. It works well for many simple gases, but not for gases consisting of more complex particles or interactions. Most of the Universe is made up of *plasma*, a gas consisting of charged particles, mostly protons and electrons. Two different particles are present. A volume of plasma is electrically neutral, but one of the constituent particles has a positive charge and the other negative, resulting in constant interactions among the particles. The kinetic theory of ideal gases does not apply to plasma, although some aspects of it carry over quite well. This does not mean that the kinetic theory is incorrect. It means it is important to know the assumptions on which a theory is based.

Newton's three laws of motion are the basis for Newtonian mechanics, also called classical mechanics. Based on common usage this sounds like a car repair shop. Here the word "mechanics" refers to the motion of objects under the influence of external forces. Although not common, it might be called Newton's theory of motion. To this can be added Newton's law of universal gravitation. These simple laws, along with a lot of mathematics, have been the foundation for three centuries of calculations of bullet, cannonball and rocket trajectories, the motion of moving parts in machines, and any other process involving motion and forces. They continue to be valuable for scientific and technological progress. Yet in the early twentieth century they were superseded by a new theory.

Newtonian mechanics is now understood to be an approximation that is accurate at speeds well below the speed of light. Einstein's special theory of relativity must be used at speeds approaching the speed of light. Likewise, special relativity and Newton's law of universal gravitation are approximations to the general theory of relativity. Newtonian theory is fine for most everyday work. Obtaining accurate distances with your smart phone or car Global Positioning System (GPS) does require the general theory of relativity, however. Also, general relativity is crucial to the cosmologists, black hole researchers, and gravitational wave researchers you may know.

Sometimes I hear or see a statement such as "I don't take that seriously. It's just a theory." As discussed above, scientific theories on the whole are well-substantiated observationally or experimentally. There are some theories that have been discarded or don't merit a high level of confidence from their respective scientific communities. Some degree of caution is warranted. The general sentiment that a theory need not be taken seriously because it is "just a theory" is incorrect, however. All theories have limitations and underlying assumptions. Even for well-established theories it's important to understand what these are.

Models

A *scientific model* is a representation of the natural world. Laboratory mice, rats, and rhesus monkeys, for example, are used as models for human biology. Another example are models built to represent complex molecules such as chlorophyll or DNA. These are *physical models* that are useful for developing and testing hypotheses.

A *conceptual model* provides a useful visualization of a physical object or process. The Bohr atom is a visualization of electron orbits around an atomic nucleus. In the study of flares on the Sun, a conceptual model is used to unify detailed observations of flares and coronal mass ejections (CMEs), a related phenomenon responsible for extreme space weather.

Mathematical models involve fitting mathematical functions to data. These models reduce a large number of data points showing a trend to a small number of variables contained in the function (called fit parameters). These functions do not necessarily contain any information about the natural world. Studying their behavior as observed data changes, however, can lead to insights about the natural world. Closely related are *statistical models*. These provide a way to determine major properties and their variance in large quantities of data.

A type of model that deserves its own category is the *computer-based model*. These models are large computer programs that simulate aspects of the natural world. This is currently a major area of development in the sciences because of the fast speeds and large memories computers now possess. The best of these use past and current information (data), results from well-established theories, mathematics and a lot of computing power to predict the future with varying degrees of success. They predict your weather, global climate, space weather, planetary and spacecraft orbits, the spread of communicable diseases, and many other phenomena. The breadth and capability of these models increases with the progression of scientific knowledge, programming and numerical methods, and computing power.

A concern with computer-based models is that they can become so complex that, even if they do successfully describe some aspect of the natural world, it is difficult to determine why they are successful. A useful model needs to be built so it is easy to determine what each component contributes to the final result.

It might be argued that everything we know about the natural world is a model. From a philosophical perspective this may be true, but well-established scientific models are backed by repeated applications of the Scientific Method. As with theories, however, it is important to understand the assumptions and limitations associated with each model.

Chapter 3
The Scholarly Side of Science

Art, civics, history, literature, music, philosophy, the sciences: these are all academic subjects. In secondary school and college classes they all require learning and memorizing information and techniques. Ideally they all encourage critical thinking. The various sciences, as academic subjects, are similar to the others in this respect, except that they may require some laboratory experience and math background. It's not surprising that many students may view science as just another collection of knowledge to be memorized.

Just as artists create new art work and writers create new literature, scientists create new knowledge about the natural world using the Scientific Method. Each individual scientist may not be focused on all aspects of the Scientific Method, but ultimately that is how new scientific knowledge is established. To obtain new results, or to test existing results, it is important to first determine what is already known. Therefore, each researcher needs to also be an accomplished scholar.

Scientific knowledge expanded rapidly in the twentieth century. As a result, in all the sciences there is a tremendous amount of information about a wide variety of topics. This information is primarily contained in journals that have increased in size and multiplied in number. For astronomy alone Wikipedia lists 69 journals (this includes astronomy, astrophysics, and space sciences). This does not include multidisciplinary journals such as *Nature* and *Science*. Related papers in astrophysics and astrobiology can also appear in journals contained in the even longer lists of physics journals and biology journals, respectively.

It has been estimated[5] that the total number of science papers published since 1665 exceeds 50 million, with 2.5 million new papers published each year in 28,000 peer reviewed journals! The estimated number of papers published per year just in astronomy and astrophysics is 25,000[6]. During most of the 20th century a scientist could read papers in his or her specialized subfield and keep up with new results in the broader field by reading review papers. That level of knowledge has mostly become a thing of the past. Beyond the general level of knowledge taught in college classes, scientists have necessarily become more specialized.

So, in testing a hypothesis, how can a scientist confidently "search for any information already available pertaining to the validity of the hypothesis and prediction"? Fortunately, most of the scientific

---

[5] Boon, S., 21st Century Science Overload (Canadian Science Publishing), January 7, 2017 (http://blog.cdnsciencepub.com/21st-century-science-overload/)

[6] Santamaria, L., Mining 50 years of astronomy and astrophysics publications data (Gender Gap in Science), March 17, 2018 (https://gender-gap-in-science.org/2018/03/17/mining-50-years-of-astronomy-and-astrophysics-publications-data/)

literature has been digitized. Scientific journals now either have an online version or are entirely online. Consequently, search engines can be used to find relevant papers. Even abstracts of papers presented orally at scientific meetings can be found online.

   Some research papers can be found with a major search engine such as Google. Databases of academic research papers and books can be searched at Google Scholar and Microsoft Academic. Many science disciplines, however, have specialized search engines that are more comprehensive and convenient for scientific research. They typically make it easy to find papers from specific periods of time and specific journals. Paper titles, abstracts, and/or main text can be searched for key words or phrases. Once relevant papers are found, previous papers cited by these papers, and later papers that cite these papers, can be located. They usually allow citations and links to papers of interest to be downloaded. These search engines facilitate, if not guarantee, a thorough search of the relevant literature.

   Access to full research articles depends on the journal. Some journals are owned by private publishers. Elsevier, for example, is a major publisher of science journals and books. Many of its journals require a subscription to obtain access to the papers they contain. If a library subscribes to the journal, papers may be accessible for reading or download directly through a search engine connected to the library. Elsevier and other publishers also have *open access* journals. Papers in these online journals are paid for by the authors, or more likely, the institution where they are employed. These papers are free to access and download.

Many papers are contained in journals published by a non-profit professional society. The American Institute of Physics (AIP), its many member societies and affiliated societies, for example, publish journals that are available by subscription. Depending on the journal, older articles may be open access or authors may have paid for their papers to be open access.

Many researchers submit versions of their papers to online ePrint archives. Such an archive for papers in physics, astrophysics, mathematics, and more, arXiv.org, is maintained by Cornell University. These are all open access papers. The caveat is that most have not been reviewed for the veracity of their contents. Many, however, are almost identical to papers that are ultimately reviewed and published. Preprint (ePrint) archives for other sciences include bioRxiv.com for biology, chemRxiv.org for chemistry, EarthArXiv.org for the earth sciences, and PsyArXiv.org for psychology.

An invaluable digital library portal and database for astrophysics research is the Astrophysics Data System (ADS). It is operated by the Smithsonian Astrophysical Observatory (SAO) under a National Aeronautics and Space Administration (NASA) cooperative agreement. You can use keywords to search for papers on a specific topic. Even specific astronomical objects can be specified using their designation in another database called SIMBAD. You can also search for papers by title or by providing an author's name. A date range can be specified for the search. Once a list of papers has been obtained, you can select a subset of these papers or bring up the title, abstract and other information about one of the papers. A link to the full paper is provided (it may not be viewable without payment or a journal subscription). It is especially valuable that references contained in the paper can be viewed without access to the full paper, as well as links to papers containing citations to the paper.

Another example of a specialized online database is PubMed.gov. It is a free database of biomedical and life sciences literature operated by the National Institutes of Health (NIH). It provides multiple ways to search for articles and books and can return a list of relevant literature. When you select a particular article it provides a list of similar articles and papers that cite the chosen article.

Wikipedia provides a list of academic databases and search engines. The free databases are clearly marked. With the tremendous growth in the number of scientists, journals, and research papers in the twentieth century, these search engines are crucial to obtaining the background knowledge necessary for properly formulating and testing a scientific hypothesis. Scientists also seek to stay current (as well as present their own work and receive feedback) by attending seminars and professional meetings. These are another valuable source of knowledge. Ultimately, however, scientific results must be archived in the reviewed and printed literature, now mostly digital.

Chapter 4
Experiments, Observations, and Instrumentation

The core of the Scientific Method is observations and experiments. Experimentation is the most desirable approach because it allows the researcher to control factors that might interfere with or confuse the outcome of the test of a hypothesis. It also allows the researcher to make controlled changes to the experiment to see how they affect the outcome. In some of the sciences only observations are possible. In these sciences the researcher, rather than devise an experiment, must devise additional observations to test a hypothesis.

Both experiments and observations ultimately depend on technology. Even the simplest scientific questions, pursued through testing a series of hypotheses, typically lead to a point where the unaided human senses are no longer adequate to make further progress. Some kind of instrumentation that extends the senses is needed.

Experimentation

Let's return to the question (Chapter 2) "Why are leaves green?" The story begins, as is often the case, with a different question. In the 1620s in what is now Belgium, Jan van Helmont wanted to know where the new material and weight come from when a tree grows. Since trees grow in soil, a reasonable working *hypothesis* is "The increasing weight of a tree as it grows comes from the soil." To test this he weighed a willow tree sapling (5 pounds) and planted it in 200 pounds of dried soil. So the relevant *prediction* was that the weight of the soil would decrease by an amount equal to the weight gained by the tree sapling. He let it grow in a pot for five years with sunlight and regular waterings. He then separately weighed the tree and the soil, after drying the soil again. The tree gained 164 pounds in weight, but the weight of the soil decreased by only about 2 ounces. He concluded that the tree's weight gain must have come from water. This leads to the new hypothesis "The increasing weight of a tree as it grows comes from water." The interpretation of this experimental result is discussed in subsequent chapters.

Even though van Helmont invented the word "gas", he gave it a rather mystical meaning and did not know that plants could absorb and emit gases. It took a century and a half for this to become established. He hypothesized the production of a gas when charcoal is burned, noting that the remaining ash is lighter than the charcoal that was burned. We now know this gas was carbon dioxide. The presence of this gas was confirmed in the 1750s by Joseph Black in Scotland.

In the early 1770s in England Joseph Priestley was performing experiments to understand air and the process of combustion. He used a bell jar to create a closed environment, isolated from the air external to the bell jar. He knew that if he put a burning candle inside the jar it would burn out well before the flame burned to the bottom of the candle. He also found that a mouse could not live long in the closed environment of the bell jar. When he placed a mint plant in the jar with a mouse, however, the mouse remained alive. This demonstrated that the plant emitted a gas that was required for the life of the mouse. In 1778 Jan Ingenhousz demonstrated that sunlight was also required. It is interesting that this experiment was repeated in England in 2012 with a sealed glass room containing plants, illuminated with external artificial lighting, and a 47 year old man for the BBC "How to Make a Planet" series[7].

In France in 1778 Antoine Lavoisier had recognized that the gas discovered by Priestley is one component of air and named it oxygen. He had carried out careful measurements that established the conservation of mass in chemical reactions and allowed individual atomic elements and molecules to be identified. Lavoisier laid the groundwork for chemistry similar to how Newton laid the groundwork for physics nearly a century earlier.

By the end of the 18th century, the Swiss naturalist Jean Senebier had established that, in the presence of light, green leaves consume carbon dioxide and emit oxygen. Entering into the 19th century, the hypothesis above from the early 17th century can be updated to "The

---

[7] Martin, D., Thompson, A., et al., A paradigm of fragile Earth in Priestley's bell jar, in Extreme Physiology & Medicine, 1: 4, 2012.

increasing weight of a tree as it grows comes from water and carbon dioxide. The carbon dioxide is absorbed by leaves in the presence of sunlight and oxygen is emitted."

The chemical responsible for the green color of leaves, chlorophyll, was chemically extracted and named in 1817. With an improved microscope and careful sample preparation for the microscope slide, in 1837 the German botanist Hugo van Mohl found that chlorophyll is isolated to discrete regions in leaf cells, later named chloroplasts. At this time all of the pieces are in place for the basic definition of photosynthesis, although this term was not coined until 1893.

This description of photosynthesis states what happens outside a leaf (input and output), but doesn't say much about what is happening within the leaf. How does the leaf convert water, carbon dioxide and sunlight to plant growth and molecular oxygen? The chemical composition and structure of chlorophyll and other relevant molecules, and the steps involved in photosynthesis, were not established until the 20th century.

In 1906, while analyzing the atomic content of the chlorophyll molecule, the German chemist Richard Willstätter found that it contained magnesium. Since neither water nor carbon dioxide contain magnesium, this implies plant growth depends on trace elements from soil. Thus although, as van Helmont found, soil makes a negligible contribution to the increasing weight of a growing tree, elements in the soil are important to the growth of the tree. In addition to carbon, hydrogen, oxygen and magnesium, chlorophyll

The Scientific Method

also contains nitrogen. Even though air contains molecular nitrogen, plants must obtain it from soil.

The full structure of chlorophyll was not determined until 1967, by the English chemist Ian Fleming. The American chemist Robert Woodward and others synthesized a version of chlorophyll in 1960 and updated the synthesized molecule in 1990. This could only be done using 20th century spectroscopic techniques and organic chemistry, and a lot of careful planning.

The chemical pathways for photosynthesis to convert water, carbon dioxide, and light to the carbohydrates required by plants are too complex to review here. A fascinating result from 20th century biochemistry is the similarity of the core of the chlorophyll molecule, which contains a single atom of magnesium, to the core of hemoglobin, which contains a single atom of iron. Hemoglobin provides the red color of blood and is crucial for transporting oxygen from the lungs to the rest of the body. The biosynthesis pathways plants and animals use to produce chlorophyll and hemoglobin, respectively, are quite similar. Both also use the molecule adenosine triphosphate (ATP) to store and transport energy. Plants and animals have more in common than meets the eye.

The primary purpose of this historical example is to illustrate the power of experimentation and quantitative measurements, as well as some limitations. As always, the first step is to ask a question and persistently seek an answer. The more difficult second step is to formulate a hypothesis that is testable. What is testable depends on current knowledge and technology.

When van Helmont asked what a tree needs to grow in the early 17th century, he concluded that he could test the hypothesis that a tree's increased weight comes from the soil. His experimental equipment consisted of a pot, soil, and a scale, as well as water, the tree sapling, and a cover to prevent loss of soil. He presumably waited five years to re-weigh the tree and dried soil to make sure the tree gained enough weight to obtain a significant result.

The correct conclusion from van Helmont's experiment is that the majority of the weight gained by the tree did not come from the soil. He hypothesized that water provided the weight gain, but he did not weigh the water, most likely because he decided he could not adequately determine the weight of water absorbed by the tree. He might have hypothesized that about two ounces of the weight of the tree did come from the soil, but this depends on being able to control the amount of soil and weigh it to an accuracy better than 2 ounces out of 200 pounds (0.06%)! It is unlikely that the measured weight lost from the soil was significant.

Van Helmont's experiment illustrates the importance of careful measurements and knowing the uncertainty in those measurements. It also illustrates the time and patience often required for a conclusive experiment. Lavoisier again demonstrated the importance of careful measurements in the late 18th century. Priestley was not so focused on quantitative measurements, but he did introduce an experimental setup for confining and studying gases. Among other things he obtained the important result that plants produce a gas that is important to animal life.

The Scientific Method

For practical academic purposes science is divided into multiple subjects. However, to obtain answers to the basic, related questions "How do plants grow?" and "Why are leaves green?" required advances in biology, chemistry, and physics.

Observations

A science that depends heavily on observations is astronomy. It is clearly not possible to reproduce planets, stars, galaxies, or the Universe in a laboratory. This does not mean that astronomy does not depend on experiments at all. Experimental results and concepts from other sciences, especially physics, are crucial to the interpretation of astronomical observations. Progress in astronomy is highly dependent on progress in technology and instrumentation.

Galileo Galilei did not invent the telescope, but he was the first to use it for astronomical observations and publish his results. He did produce telescopes with available lenses that provided relatively poor images, but the images were upright with magnifications as high as 30x. His famous observations of features on the Moon, the phases of Venus, the brightest moons of Jupiter, the rings of Saturn, and stars in the Milky Way were first published in 1610. These observations helped refute concepts of a geometrically simple Universe with Earth at the center. (For the curious, an easily assembled Galilean telescope can currently be purchased for $79.99 USD[8].)

---

[8] Explore Scientific Galileoscope (https://explorescientificusa.com/products/galileoscope)

The first reflecting telescope was built by Isaac Newton in 1668. Larger diameter telescopes collect more light and, therefore, can observe dimmer objects in the sky. They also have greater resolving power — they are able to display finer details. Since large focusing mirrors are lighter and more compact than telescopes based entirely on lenses (refractors), most telescopes for both professional and amateur astronomers are reflectors. Newton was able to verify and improve on Galileo's observations with his reflector.

In the late 17th century comets became an important test of Newton's theoretical work. A small telescope was used by Gottfried Kirch to observe and track a comet for the first time in 1680. Comets were also observed and tracked in 1681 and 1682. These observations became a test of the hypothesis "Newton's laws of motion and gravity, together with mathematics, can be used to determine the orbit and period of a comet."

The first Astronomer Royal of England, John Flamsteed, had made detailed observations of stars and their locations in the sky. He also made observations of the location of the 1680 and 1681 comets and their change in position with time. He hypothesized that these were the same comet, seen before and after orbiting around the Sun. His data were obtained by Edmond Halley, who later became the second Astronomer Royal. Halley and Isaac Newton used Newton's methods to compute the comet's orbit, verifying Flamsteed's hypothesis.

Halley also computed the orbit and period of the 1682 comet. In addition to the gravitational force of the Sun, he also estimated the impact of the gravitational force from the two massive planets

Jupiter and Saturn on the orbit. He concluded that comets observed in 1531 and 1607 were the same comet and predicted that the comet would be observed again in 1758. He did not live to see that his prediction was correct, but after this appearance it became known as Halley's Comet.

In the late 18th century Charles Messier and Pierre Méchain sought to discover comets in the sky above Paris using a four inch refracting telescope. They produced a catalog of fixed, diffuse objects to avoid misidentifying them as comets. The resulting Messier catalog, containing a total of 110 objects designated M1 - M110, provides a compendium of interesting objects observable with small telescopes.

After significant improvements in both lenses and mirror surfaces, large telescopes started to be built in the late 18th century. Between 1785 and 1789 the brother and sister musicians William (Friedrich Wilhelm) and Caroline Lucretia Herschel, immigrants from Hanover (Germany) to England, built a 49.5 inch diameter reflecting telescope. Because of its impressive length (and focal length), it became known as the Great Forty-Foot Telescope. In addition to other achievements, they published a catalog of 2500 nebulae (fixed, diffuse objects) and star clusters. This catalog was expanded by John Herschel, William's son, to become the New General Catalog (NGC) of interesting astronomical objects. The telescope was funded by King George III, who made William court astronomer and paid Caroline a stipend as his assistant. This apparently made Caroline the first woman to be paid as an astronomer and the first woman to be given a government position in England.

In order to study in greater detail the nebulae cataloged by Messier and the Herschels, William Parsons, the third Earl of Rosse, built a 72 inch diameter reflecting telescope at Birr Castle in Ireland. Built from 1842 to 1845, this 54 feet long, 12 ton telescope became known as the "Leviathan of Parsonstown". Both the Herschels' large telescope and Lord Rosse's telescope, built with help from his wife Mary Field Parsons, the Countess of Rosse, attracted considerable interest and visitors. An important discovery with the "Leviathan" was the observation that some nebulae have a spiral structure.

A minor but interesting example of the importance of knowing how experimental and observational results are obtained, and of verifying them with additional experiments or observations, is Lord Rosse's drawing of the first nebula in the Messier catalog, M1. Observed with a telescope half the diameter of the Leviathan, his drawing of it reminded him of a crab, so he named it the Crab Nebula. When he observed it later with the Leviathan, the crab structure was no longer apparent. The nebula is now understood to be the remnant of a supernova that exploded in 1054. Despite its revised structure, this highly studied astronomical object is still known as the Crab Nebula.

Of crucial importance to progress in astronomy and other sciences was the discovery and development of line spectroscopy. Isaac Newton described how a glass prism refracts light so that it is dispersed into the rainbow of colors contained in the spectrum of visible white light or sunlight. In the early 19th century Joseph von Fraunhofer developed spectroscopes with greater clarity and

The Scientific Method

dispersion than Newton's prism. He found that the spectrum of the Sun contains hundreds of dark lines with fixed positions. He also examined the spectra of some bright stars and found that they also contained dark lines, but not all in the same positions as those in the Sun's spectrum.

By the middle of the 19th century it became clear from experiments by scientists such as Gustav Kirchhoff and Robert Bunsen that low-density, hot gases emit spectral lines that can be used to identify the atomic elements in a gas. The dark lines observed by Fraunhofer were these same lines seen in absorption. The relatively low-density, cool gas at the surface of the Sun or another star absorbs the continuous spectrum of emission from the star at the locations of the lines seen in the emitted spectra of the same hot gases.

Equally important to progress in astronomy was the discovery and verification of the Doppler effect. It was proposed in Prague in 1842 by Christian Doppler and independently proposed in Paris in 1848 by Hippolyte Fizeau. The hypothesis states that when a source of sound or light is moving relative to an observer, the observer experiences a shift in the frequency of the radiation that is proportional to the relative speed. The pitch (frequency) of a car horn or train whistle will be higher than the emitted pitch as the vehicle approaches and lower as the vehicle moves away. For light, the radiation from an object moving toward you will be shifted toward higher frequencies (blue shifted) and the radiation from an object moving away from you will be shifted toward lower frequencies (red shifted). (Note that for the speeds at which a car or train travels, the Doppler shift of light would not be perceptible to the eye.) Despite the construction by the Austrian physicist Ernst Mach of experimental apparatuses demonstrating the Doppler effect for sound, the hypothesis was not broadly accepted in the scientific community until it was clearly identified in spectra from stars.

Christian Doppler's hypothesis for light lacked verification until 1868, fifteen years after his death in 1853. The English astronomer William Huggins reported that the absorption lines in the spectrum of the bright star Sirius were red shifted. Even more definitive, in 1872 the German astronomer Hermann Vogel measured the maximum red and blue shifts along the equator of the Sun and found that the velocities corresponding to these Doppler shifts were consistent with the rotation rate of the Sun deduced from the motion of sunspots[9].

In 1864 William Huggins showed that some "nebulae" have emission lines in their spectra while others, like individual stars, have absorption line spectra. This confirmed that not all of these objects are just unresolved clusters of stars. He and his wife, astronomer Margaret Lindsay Huggins, later used newly developed dry plate photography to record the spectra of astronomical objects.

Another crucial but difficult step in astronomy was determining the distance to objects. The most direct way to deduce the distance to a far-away object is parallax, the change in the apparent position of an object relative to much more distant objects as you change the position from which you observe the nearer object. If you change

---

[9] Nolte, David D., The Fall and Rise of the Doppler Effect, Physics Today, Vol. 73, No. 3, page 30, March, 2020.

your position perpendicular to the direction to a distant tree, its position relative to objects on the horizon changes. The closer the tree, the greater the apparent change in position relative to the more distant objects. By measuring the distance you moved and the change in angle at which you see the tree, you can deduce the distance to the tree. Our brain uses the parallax angle of the relative position of objects seen by our two eyes to provide us with depth perception.

Parallax is used to deduce the distance to relatively nearby stars and other astronomical objects. In 189 B. C. Hipparchus used parallax and the timing of a solar eclipse at two locations on Earth to estimate the distance to the moon. The first use of parallax to deduce the distance to a star (other than our Sun) was not until 1838, by Friedrich Bessel. Stars are so distant that even the closest have a parallax angle of less than one second of arc (one 3,600th of a degree). Astronomical parallax is measured using the longest practical distance between observations, the diameter of Earth's orbit around the Sun. The second observation of the position of the star is made six months after the first. Bessel had the technology (and patience) to determine that the star is about 11 light years away. (One light year is the distance light travels in one year.)

Most astronomical objects are too far away to have measurable parallax. Fortunately, a clever alternative was discovered in 1908 by Henrietta Leavitt at Harvard College Observatory. She was studying multiple photographs of stars for which the brightness had been observed to change with time. The photographs were obtained with Harvard College's 24 inch diameter refracting telescope in Peru. The variable stars were located in two large groups of stars in the southern hemisphere sky called the Magellanic clouds. Called Cepheid variables, the brightness (and temperature) of these stars oscillates with a period ranging from days to months. Leavitt found that the brighter the star, the longer the period of oscillation. Since the stars were in the same group, she concluded that they were all about the same distance away. This implies that the intrinsic brightness, or luminosity, of Cepheid variables increases with increasing period.

The observed brightness of an unresolved light source such as a distant star decreases with the distance from the observer to the source. Specifically, it decreases as one over distance squared, since the emitted light spreads out over the surface of a sphere that has a greater surface area at greater distances. (The surface area of a sphere is proportional to the square of its radius.) Therefore, if the observed brightness and intrinsic brightness of a star are both known, the distance to the star can be calculated. Once the period and brightness of a Cepheid variable are measured, its distance can be determined using the period-luminosity relationship. The only problem was that the distance to the Magellanic clouds was not known, so only relative distance could be determined.

The parallax angle and, therefore, distance to several Cepheid variable stars was measured in 1918. Unfortunately, these distances were substantially incorrect. Nevertheless, this work led to the development of a "cosmic distance ladder" that provided a way to deduce the distance to far-away stars and nebulae. These distance determinations have been and continue to be improved, revised and refined as an important ongoing component of astronomical research.

The development of this cosmic distance ladder and the measurement of stellar and nebular Doppler shifts led to our modern concept of the Universe. At the beginning of the 20th century little was known about the size of the Universe and the location of our Solar System within it. The existence of the Milky Way and Galileo's observation that it is made up of many individual stars supports the hypothesis that our Solar System is located in a flattened disk of stars. Astronomers did not know whether all of the nebulae were also associated with this disk, making it the full extent of the Universe, or whether at least some of the nebulae were more distant and much larger. In 1920 the Smithsonian Museum of Natural History sponsored a debate on this topic. This did not resolve the issue, of course, since scientific hypotheses are not established through debate.

In 1912 - 1914 at Lowell Observatory in Arizona the American astronomer Vesto Slipher measured the Doppler shifts of 15 of the nebulae that showed spiral structure. He showed that these flattened nebulae were rotating and that all showed redshifts. Therefore, they were all moving away from our Solar System.

In 1917 a 100 inch diameter reflecting telescope was completed at Mount Wilson Observatory in California. This telescope was largely funded by John D. Hooker and Andrew Carnegie. Using this telescope, Edwin Hubble in 1923 discovered a Cepheid variable star in the Andromeda spiral nebula. Using its observed brightness and period, and its inferred luminosity, its distance was found to be much greater than the distance to stars within the Milky Way. Cepheids were subsequently discovered in other spiral nebulae, all indicating distances much greater than the distances to stars and nebulae in the Milky Way. It became apparent that the Milky way is one of many spiral galaxies in a universe that is much larger than the extent of our own Milky Way galaxy.

Hubble and, independently, the Belgian priest and scientist Georges Lemaître compared the deduced galaxy distances to their measured redshifts and found that more distant galaxies have larger redshifts. This relationship is now called the Hubble-Lemaître Law. It provides a way to determine the distance to faraway galaxies by measuring their redshifts. It also has the profound implication that the Universe is expanding. Lemaître showed that this law is predicted by a solution to Einstein's General Theory of Gravitation. These results from the late 1920s provide the basis for our current understanding of the origin and evolution of the Universe, the Big Bang Theory.

Astronomical observations have benefitted not only from the technological ability to build larger and larger optical telescopes, but also from the ability to observe the Universe at radiation frequencies outside the the frequency range visible to the human eye. Celestial radio waves were first detected in 1932. Like optical telescopes, radio telescopes have become larger and technologically more sophisticated. These radio telescopes opened up a whole new view of the Universe.

Space programs have also expanded astronomical horizons. Most radiation outside the visible frequencies does not get through Earth's

The Scientific Method

atmosphere to ground level. Detectors mounted on balloons, rockets, and satellites have made it possible to observe high-energy ultraviolet, X-ray, and gamma-ray emissions from astronomical objects, including our own Sun and Solar System and hot gas both within and in the space between galaxies.

Observations from above most of Earth's atmosphere can improve observations in the visible (and near-visible) range as well. This is demonstrated by the beautiful images and other data from NASA's Hubble Space Telescope. Thanks to low background light and low atmospheric distortion, it views dimmer objects and obtains higher resolution images than would have been possible for the same telescope at Earth's surface.

Infrared radiation is emitted between the radio and visible light frequencies. Extending the Hubble-Lemaître Law to great distances, objects that emit most of their light at visible frequencies will be seen by us as redshifted into the infrared. Since radiation emitted from further away will take longer to reach us, these objects will also be older. Therefore, observing objects in the infrared allows us to view the Universe at an earlier age. Also, nearer stars, nebulae and other objects that are cooler than those emitting primarily visible light radiate mostly in the infrared. The recently launched great astronomical space observatory, the James Webb Space Telescope, observes primarily in the infrared. It was launched on 2021 December 25.

Chapter Summary

All scientific hypotheses must be shown to be acceptable or rejected through observations of the natural world. An acceptable hypothesis is one that has been tested and not rejected and is useful for making further scientific progress. It can still possibly be shown to be incorrect. An observation is an experiment when the system being observed can be controlled and changed by the researcher. The observed system is typically an apparatus or contained within an apparatus created by the researcher, such as Priestly's bell jar experiments. In van Helmont's willow tree experiment, the apparatus was simply a pot, and a scale for weighing the tree and the soil in which it grew. The system being observed in sciences such as epidemiology and clinical research can be different groups of people experiencing different conditions or drugs controlled by the researcher.

Progress in science and technology are interconnected. The growth of scientific knowledge leads to more sophisticated technology. In turn, new technology leads to more sophisticated instrumentation for experiments and making observations.

I included dates in this chapter to show that scientific progress is not as reliable or rapid as it might appear to be from a quick, academic synopsis. It is not unusual for a decade or more to pass before a hypothesis is found to be acceptable and receives general acceptance in the relevant scientific community.

Science is and should always be an international affair. This is reflected in the nationalities of the scientists included here. The importance of an active scientific community and open, frequent communications among these scientists is discussed in Chapter 6.

Chapter 5
The Importance of Simplicity

This chapter focuses on the choice of a hypothesis. During the process of seeking answers to a question, it is likely that you will come up with multiple hypotheses to be tested. Which one should you choose? You could attempt to test all of them, but that could take considerable time. A sensible answer would be to start with a hypothesis that is relatively easy to test. Also, you may have a preferred hypothesis, one you consider most likely to be acceptable. Before making this decision, however, it is important to assess your hypotheses on the basis of simplicity.

Simplicity is not an issue that is usually considered when describing the Scientific Method. It is quite important, however. A simpler hypothesis is preferred over a more complex hypothesis. You might be inclined to object to this statement, arguing that the natural world is complex and, therefore, the simpler hypothesis should not be given any preference. It is true that the world is complex and the simplest hypothesis is not always the correct one. Nevertheless, the simplest hypothesis is the one that should be chosen. Why? And what do I mean by "simplest"?

One of the greatest strengths of the Scientific Method is that the knowledge and insights it provides can lead to basic principles that apply to a wide variety of systems and situations. Famous major examples of this in physics, touched upon elsewhere in this book, are Newton's and Einstein's laws of motion, relativity, and gravitation. These basic principles are more readily identified from a search for simple hypotheses. A valid scientific hypothesis is simpler than another if it requires fewer assumptions. For a mathematical model, this means fewer variables are required to describe the relevant data. Equally important, compared to a more complex hypothesis, a simpler hypothesis is easier to test and potentially demonstrate to be unacceptable.

Let's return to van Helmont's hypothesis (Chapter 4) that the increasing weight of a tree as it grows comes from the soil. He might have hypothesized that it comes from water. This hypothesis has the weakness, however, that it would have been difficult to test. Keeping track of the amount of water that reached the tree and the amount of water lost from the pot over five years would have been prohibitively difficult. On the other hand, the weight of soil in the pot could be will controlled. He might have also hypothesized that the weight of the tree came from the combination of soil and water. The test of this hypothesis would have required weighing wet soil and suffers from the same difficulties as testing the hypothesis that the weight gain came from water alone. The experiment would not provide information about the weight gained from water alone or soil alone.

Van Helmont's hypothesis is simple in that it is a clear, focused statement that does not depend on any significant untested assumptions. It was the simplest hypothesis because it could be tested with a relatively simple experiment that could give a clear, unambiguous answer. The experiment clearly demonstrated that the hypothesis is false. Even though the result was negative, it was significant progress in understanding plants and their growth. In science, negative results are often as valuable as positive ones.

I noted in the previous chapter that van Helmont concluded that the weight gained by the tree sapling must have come from water. Based on the result of his experiment, this is not a valid conclusion. The correct conclusion from his experiment is that the increase in the weight of the sapling did not significantly originate from the soil. The word "significantly" is here because his result does not rule out the possibility that some small amount of the weight gain did come from the soil. This is discussed in the next chapter. The hypothesis and experimental test only demonstrate that the soil was not responsible for most of the weight gain. They provide no information about the actual source of the weight gained by the tree.

It is important to note here that the question of the source of the weight gained by trees (and plants in general) contains implicit assumptions that needed to be tested. One is generalizing the result for one tree to all plants (inductive reasoning). The hypothesis that all plants gain weight in the same way as the one examined in an experiment needed to be tested for many plants. This cannot be done for all individual plants, of course. The scientific method states that a hypothesis is acceptable until it is demonstrated to be incorrect. This approach is a crucial step in allowing us to increase our understanding of the natural world.

Another important underlying assumption is that when one thing gains weight, one or more things must lose an equal amount of weight. This is also a scientific hypothesis that needed to be tested. This hypothesis, now the law of conservation of mass (mass instead of weight, because weight depends on the local force of gravity), was not adequately tested until the experiments of Lavoisier, a century and a half after van Helmont's experiment. If van Helmont's experiment had shown that the soil decreased in weight by an amount equal to the weight gain of the tree sapling, it would have been a test of conservation of mass.

The salient point here is that as a scientific discipline develops, new hypotheses are built on previously tested hypotheses. The test of a hypothesis tests both it and all underlying hypotheses upon which it may depend. Therefore, it is important that the underlying hypotheses are known and have been scientifically verified. Otherwise, the interpretation of the experimental or observational result is compromised, or at least confused, by the uncertainty in any underlying hypothesis.

The concept of choosing the simplest hypothesis is generally referred to as Occam's razor (also spelled Ockham's or Ocham's). In the early 14th century the English Franciscan friar William of Ockham wrote that "plurality must never be posited without necessity". A similar comment attributed to him is "Entities must not be multiplied beyond necessity." Hence, if you imagine shaving away unnecessary assumptions and complexity, the term "Occam's razor" becomes meaningful. Despite its apparent simplicity, this concept has been analyzed, discussed, and elaborated on over the centuries. This concept is also known as the principle of *parsimony,* where the word parsimony alludes to stinginess with assumptions.

I have seen the statement that Occam's razor is applied in science because of the belief that the simplest hypothesis is usually the correct hypothesis. This statement is incorrect. More commonly, Occam's razor is thought of as an optional additional consideration, independent of the scientific method. This is also incorrect. The purpose of science is to understand the natural world. As discussed previously, a valid scientific hypothesis needs to provide a prediction that is testable with an experiment or observation. Whether the hypothesis is found to be acceptable or false, progress has been made in answering the scientific question that inspired the hypothesis. If the hypothesis is complex with multiple components or underlying untested hypotheses, a clear, unambiguous answer will be difficult if not impossible to obtain.

The goal of science is to understand the natural world in terms of simple principles. It may be logically or mathematically complex to describe many phenomena and formulate predictions, but these descriptions and predictions are based on simple principles. This simplicity allows us to understand how and why natural phenomena exist or occur. A complex hypothesis may appear to be acceptable, but the question of why it is acceptable remains open. Simplicity is at the heart of science.

An important historic example of the impact of inadequately tested hypotheses on a model and on the progress of science is Ptolemy's model of our Solar System. Recorded observations of the motion of the visible planets relative to fixed background stars go back to at least the ancient Sumerians (roughly 2000 BC). The planets normally move eastward with respect to the background stars. At times, however, they reverse direction and move westward. This observed change in direction is called retrograde motion. These strange reversals in direction of motion, along with the more obvious occurrence of solar and lunar eclipses and the phases of the moon, fueled the desire for an explanation as well as a desire to be able to predict future planetary locations and eclipses.

Around 150 AD Claudius Ptolemy released the first comprehensive model of our Solar System. (At that time in history, a model of the Universe!) His model placed Earth at the center of the Universe, stationary with no orbital or spinning motions. The Moon, Sun, and planets follow circular orbits. The orbits around Earth were called *deferents*. In order to explain the observed retrograde motion, each planet moved around another circle, called an *epicycle*, that moved around the deferent. In this model the Moon had the closest orbit (deferent) to Earth, followed by Mercury, Venus, the Sun, Mars, Jupiter, and Saturn. The fixed stars were on a great sphere beyond the orbit of Saturn. The entire external Universe spun around Earth to provide daily motion across the sky.

In order to adequately explain and predict the motions of the planets, Moon, and Sun, the center of the deferents had to be shifted away from the center of Earth and, therefore, the center of the Universe. Previous models assumed each object or epicycle moved with constant speed around its circular deferent. Ptolemy had to modify this assumption. He introduced another point, not located at the center of the deferent, from which the motion of the object or epicycle would be seen to have constant speed. This point was called the *equant*. Hence the concept of constant speed around a circle was maintained, but not around the deferent.

All of these hypotheses are now known to be incorrect. Earth is not stationary or at the center of the Solar System. The planets, Sun and the Moon do not follow circular orbits. They do not have a constant speed around an equant point. Nevertheless, Ptolemy's model was sufficiently flexible that it provided acceptable results for fifteen centuries! If a prediction started to vary from subsequent observations, the model could be adjusted by shifting a position or adding more epicycles.

In 1543 the Polish astronomer Nicolaus Copernicus published a model with the Sun at its center (a *heliocentric* model) that provided significant simplifications compared to Ptolemy's model. The ordering of the planets was similar to that of Ptolemy's model, except that Earth is located between the orbits of Venus and Mars and the Moon orbits Earth. In addition to orbiting the Sun, Earth spins to provide the daily cycle of the Sun and objects in the sky seen from Earth. Its spin axis is tilted to explain seasonal changes. His model still featured circular deferents with constant speed around each. Epicycles were still needed to correct for these assumptions. On the other hand, he realized that he could dispense with the equant points. Retrograde motion was explained by the orbital motion of Earth relative to the orbital motion of the other planets, removing the need for epicycles to explain this phenomenon.

Copernicus' model also provided a natural explanation for the *greatest elongations* of Mercury and Venus relative to the Sun without requiring epicycles. The angular distance (*elongation*) of these planets from the Sun in the sky is limited so that they are never seen high above the horizon at night. The location of their orbits inside Earth's orbit provides a natural explanation for this.

Scientifically, Copernicus' model is simpler than that of Ptolemy's because it explains multiple observations with less complexity. The addition of epicycles is not necessary to explain retrograde motion or the greatest elongation of the inner planets Mercury and Venus. Earth spins instead of the entire external Universe to explain daily motion, and the tilt of Earth's spin axis explains seasonal changes and why they differ in the northern and southern hemispheres. Copernicus' heliocentric model explains *why* several phenomena are observed in terms of a relatively simple planetary model, while Ptolemy's *geocentric* model requires extra orbits (the epicycles) to force the model to produce these observed phenomena.

Fearing ridicule and possible condemnation for proposing a model other than that which had been used and taught for centuries, Copernicus did not publish his heliocentric model until the year of his death. It took another century before the heliocentric model was widely accepted. A major change that eventually led to this acceptance was new technology: the telescope and Galileo's use of it to observe celestial objects. As discussed in the previous chapter, his observations revealed moons orbiting the planet Jupiter, a ring around Saturn, and the phases of Venus, and other features that helped erode belief in the special position of Earth at the center of the Universe.

A concern about the heliocentric model was the belief that if Earth were moving or spinning, the atmosphere and all loose objects on Earth's surface would have been flung off by the motion. Galileo's hypothesis that, in the absence of an external impediment (force), a moving body on a level or spherical surface will maintain itself in that movement, provided a possible alternative to that belief. A modified version of this hypothesis became Newton's First Law of motion (inertia) in the second half of the seventeenth century.

The simplicity of Copernicus' model inspired the German mathematician and astronomer (and astrologer!) Johannes Kepler to analyze the best available planetary data in terms of the heliocentric model. From this analysis he was able to identify three laws. The first is that the planets have elliptical orbits with the Sun at a focus of the ellipse. The second is that the area swept out by a line between the Sun and the planet as it orbits around the Sun is equal for equal periods of time. Since the orbit is not circular, this means the speed of the planet in its orbit is not constant. These two laws remove the remaining epicycles from the heliocentric model. The third law is that the period of time it takes the planet to completely orbit the Sun *squared* is proportional to the maximum distance of the planet from the Sun (formally, the semi-major axis of the ellipse) *cubed*. These three laws gave rise to the immensely valuable scientific question: Why? Why do planetary orbits obey these three simple laws?

The search for an answer to this question contributed to a revolution in the field of physics. In 1687 Isaac Newton published his three laws of motion and his universal law of gravity. From these simple laws he was able to derive Kepler's laws and much more.

They remain the foundation for the physics of how objects move and interact (classical mechanics), modified in the early twentieth century by Einstein's work on relativity and gravitation.

All scientific models are based on simpler hypotheses. To evaluate a model, it is important to know what these hypotheses are. It is then important to evaluate the validity of these hypotheses. If one or more of these hypotheses is not well established, application of the model to observations is a test of the hypotheses that have not been validated. It is difficult to evaluate a model that contains multiple hypotheses that are not well established. It is even more difficult if these hypotheses are not simple.

We have seen that a model can be useful in a practical sense, even if some or all of its underlying hypotheses are incorrect. The fact that Ptolemy's geocentric model needed constant tweaking was evidence that it was fundamentally flawed. The price of constantly making these tweaks instead of reexamining the underlying hypotheses was centuries of stagnation in the physical sciences. Simple, testable hypotheses are essential to progress in the sciences.

Models are important because the natural world is often not simple. Observed phenomena are typically the result of a combination of multiple forces and physical properties. Models provide a way to test our understanding of these observed phenomena and make predictions for future observations or experiments. Like hypotheses, models can be rejected or modified as required by experimental or observational results. Models are more easily corrected by small modifications than simple hypotheses, however, because of their complexity. It is important to always be cognizant of the hypotheses upon which a model is based, as well as what information or hypotheses are not included in the model. If the focus is not on testing and understanding the impact of these simpler, underlying hypotheses when applying a model, the model can inhibit rather than contribute to scientific progress.

Chapter 6
Science is a Group Activity

Now that you have settled on a hypothesis and a way to test it, studied the literature for existing information about the subject, carried out your experiment or observations, and decided whether it is acceptable or unacceptable, the next step is to make your results public. This is an important step regardless of whether you find the hypothesis to be acceptable or incorrect. Scientific knowledge advances only if you and others contribute to and update the literature you study before testing your hypothesis.

It is not sufficient to simply report your *conclusion*. How you reached that conclusion is just as important as the conclusion itself. Ideally, your report should contain a *clear statement of your hypothesis* and a discussion of why it is important and/or interesting. It should contain a brief discussion of and *references* to existing knowledge related to your hypothesis. It should then give a clear description of how you tested the hypothesis and the *relevant details of your experiment or observations*. Then report your conclusion and how it follows from your test results. It is always helpful if the report ends with a *discussion* of studies you intend to do in the near future or others might do to further advance this particular scientific field.

Scientific papers typically begin with a short *abstract*. It is important because it is used by others to decide if they are going to read the rest of your paper. It is worth the effort to make your abstract clear, informative, and interesting. The *title* of your paper should reflect its contents as precisely as possible with only a small number of words. Since search engines are often used to discover and locate scientific papers, a well-chosen set of *keywords* can also be valuable.

As discussed in Chapter 3, scientific papers are typically published in journals that specialize in the discipline relevant to the topic of research. Most journals have a website with a page providing instructions for authors. This includes styles particular to that journal and how to submit a paper. An editor decides if the paper is appropriate for the journal and typically sends it out to one or two referees who the editor deems to be qualified to evaluate the paper. The referee (or referees) comments on the paper and makes suggestions for changes or additions. This may require several iterations and the referee may have a significant impact on the version of the paper that is ultimately published. On rare occasions the referee may recommend that the paper be rejected. (Rare because the authors and the referee are usually qualified professionals with expertise in the subject.) In this case the authors may be able to request another referee.

As an area of scientific inquiry evolves, the questions and hypotheses become more specialized and the instruments and experiments required to test them become more sophisticated. For example, our seemingly simple question "Why are leaves green?" led to the question "What is the chemical structure of chlorophyll?" As a result, it becomes difficult or impossible for a single scientist to answer the question. Scientists working in these highly developed areas tend to specialize in certain aspects of the inquiry. Some focus on developing specialized instruments and experiments. Others focus on developing mathematical and computer-based models. Still others focus on understanding and interpreting the response of scientific instruments. Consequently, research articles are likely to have multiple authors, with the first author primarily responsible for the contents of the paper.

Many research papers do not follow the full Scientific Method because of this specialization. There are many useful papers that do not provide a scientific hypothesis or a test of one. Also, the Scientific Method may not be explicitly emphasized in science courses in primary schools and colleges. Today, formulating and testing a scientific hypothesis can typically require the skills of a scientist, a mathematician, a statistician, a computer programmer, an engineer, a technician, and a writer. Individual scientists often apply all of these skills to some extent. Large projects can only be accomplished with a dedicated, diverse team of experts, however. Consequently, people working in a scientific field may not be able to give a clear, complete description of the Scientific Method, giving the impression that it is not followed or does not even exist. This impression is far from the truth. No conclusion about the natural world can be found acceptable or achieve a high level of plausibility without the scrutiny of the Scientific Method.

Today many scientists work at or are otherwise associated with large experimental facilities or observatories that were not built to test only a specific hypothesis. Examples are the James Webb Space Telescope and most other astronomical observatories, CERN in Switzerland (and France) for the study of the physics of fundamental particles, the International Thermonuclear Experimental Reactor (ITER) in France, and the International Human Genome Sequencing Consortium. Facilities such as these are developed with the expertise of many people and enable scientific research that could not be undertaken by an individual scientist.

Many large experimental or observational facilities are partially or fully funded by government agencies. Scientists who do not directly work at one of these facilities can often make use of them by submitting a research proposal to the facility management or to the funding agency. These proposals are often in competition with proposals from other scientists. It is therefore important that the proposed experiment or observation be compelling and clearly described. Employment at an appropriate university, government agency, or industrial laboratory is also likely to be a consideration.

In addition to employment, most scientists need additional grant money to support their research. These grants are usually obtained by submitting proposals to government agencies such as the National Science Foundation (NSF), the National Institutes of Health (NIH), the National Aeronautics and Space Administration (NASA), or the European Space Agency (ESA). This funding typically lasts one to three years before another proposal must be submitted. Some research groups may be funded for a longer period of time. These proposals are often evaluated by other scientists who may also be seeking funding from the same agency. They are usually anonymous, but an additional committee of reviewers may know their identities. Competition for this grant money can be quite stiff. The ability to write a clear, compelling proposal with a well thought out plan of research is one of the talents scientists must master.

 A major way scientists communicate and discuss their work is by attending conferences. These can be large, such as an annual meeting of an entire professional society, or relatively small, focusing on a specialized range of topics. Typically, individual scientists submit either a short oral presentation with slides or a poster presentation for the meeting. The oral presentations are ten to fifteen minutes long with a few minutes for questions from the audience. There are usually also longer, invited oral presentations. The posters presentations may be up for viewing all day and in many cases can be multimedia. The poster presentations are most effective when sufficient time is allocated for viewing them, with no simultaneous sessions of oral presentations, and an author of the poster is present. They provide time for discussions with individual scientists.

 Scientific research has no national or cultural boundaries. Consequently, scientists generally have the opportunity to be world travelers. Travel is important for keeping abreast of advancements in a scientific field, especially considering the time required for a scientific publication to be written, evaluated and published. The exchange of ideas at conferences provides important impetus for new research, as well as being part of the evaluation process. Video conferencing provides a way for scientists anywhere in the world to collaborate and exchange ideas. For maintaining a broad, up-to-date perspective of a field and encouraging serendipitous, productive collaborations, there is no substitute for large, in person gatherings of scientists.

Chapter 7
How Much Do You Believe a Hypothesis? Give me a Number!

Testing a hypothesis usually means making one or more measurements. The *uncertainty* in these measurements is just as important as the measurement itself. If the uncertainty is sufficiently small, the case for supporting or rejecting a hypothesis can be quite strong. If the uncertainty is large, however, the case is weaker and may not be a meaningful test at all.

As an example, I return to van Helmont's tree sapling experiment discussed in Chapter 4. He planted a 5 pound willow sapling in 200 pounds of soil. After 5 years the sapling gained 164 pounds and the soil was found to be 2 ounces lighter than its original 200 pounds. This leads to the strong conclusion that most or all of the weight gained by the sapling did not come from the soil. However, the soil did decrease in weight by 2 ounces. (Only 0.06% of the original weight of the soil!) Could van Helmont have also concluded that a small amount of soil did contribute to the increased weight of the sapling?

The answer to this question depends on the uncertainty in the weight measurements. If the weight measurements could be done to within half and ounce (or better), so van Helmont could confidently argue that the weight lost by the soil was between 1.5 ounces and 2.5 ounces, it would be plausible to hypothesize that about 2 ounces of the soil contributed to the increased weight of the sapling. The strength of this hypothesis also depends on the experimental procedure. Two ounces of soil might have been lost to the wind or in the transfer of the soil to the scale. If, on the other hand, the weight of the soil could confidently be determined to within 2 ounces only (or worse), so the lost weight could likely be between 0 ounces or 4 ounces, the plausibility of the conclusion that a small amount of soil contributed to the weight of the sapling is low. Quite reasonably, van Helmont did not come to this conclusion, although the hypothesis that some of the weight of plants comes from the soil certainly merited future testing.

Another example discussed in Chapter 4 is parallax, used to determine the distance to the nearest stars. The angular resolution of the naked human eye is about one minute of arc (one sixtieth of a degree). The practical resolution of a typical optical telescope is on the order of a second of arc (one 3600th of a degree). On the other hand, the parallax of the nearest star to our Solar System, Proxima Centauri, is 0.768 seconds of arc. Therefore, its annual motion in the sky due to parallax cannot be detected with the human eye and is difficult to detect with an optical telescope. Instruments did not have the *resolving power* to provide the level of *precision* required to measure stellar parallaxes until the careful measurements of Bessel and others in the nineteenth century.

The Scientific Method

Parallax measurements clearly showed that Ptolemy's hypothesis that all stars are equidistant from the Sun (Chapter 5) is incorrect. They are a low rung of the astronomical distance ladder, with higher rungs measuring greater distances dependent on the lower rungs (Chapter 4). From 1989 to 1993 the European Space Agency's *Hipparcos* satellite measured the parallax of about 120,000 stars with an uncertainty of 0.001 seconds of arc (on the order of 10%), and about 2.5 million stars with somewhat greater uncertainty. The *Gaia* satellite, launched in December, 2013, is obtaining parallax and, therefore, distance measurements with even greater precision and lower uncertainty (as low as 0.001%). This may seem like overkill, but understanding the physical properties of stars and other astronomical objects depends on determining their distances. These improved parallax measurements propagate up the astronomical distance ladder to a better understanding of more distant objects and their motions. These *astrometric* observatories have also provided valuable information about the systematic motion of stars and their brightnesses.

A twentieth century example of the importance of knowing the uncertainty in measurements was the first test of Einstein's theory of gravity: the predicted bending of the path of light by the gravitational field of the Sun. The astrometric observations were made in 1919 during a total solar eclipse so that the relative position of stars could be measured near the limb (visible edge) of the Sun.

As described by John Taylor[10], Einstein's theory predicts a relative shift of 1.8 seconds of arc while Newton's theory predicts a shift of 0.9 seconds of arc. A stellar shift of about 2 seconds of arc was measured with a confidence interval range (uncertainty) of 1.7 to 2.3 seconds of arc. Hence the result supports Einstein's theory and is inconsistent with the shift computed from Newton's theory. This result was critical to the acceptance of Einstein's theory of gravity (also known as general relativity). It would not have been convincing without the carefully estimated interval of confidence.

The qualitative question "How much do you believe this hypothesis?" can be rephrased as the quantitative question "What is the probability this hypothesis is true?". The answer "0%" means you have found it to be false. If you're not sure, the answer is "50%". If you're absolutely sure it is true, the answer is "100%". For a scientific hypothesis the answer is never 100%, since a scientific hypothesis cannot be proven to be absolutely true (Chapter 2). A hypothesis may be so well tested, however, that your answer may be very close to 100%. For comparing alternative hypotheses, this quantification in terms of probabilities can be quite useful.

"If your experiment needs statistics, you ought to have done a better experiment." This quote (and some variations of this wording) has been attributed to the physicist Ernest Rutherford (1871 - 1937). An important part of designing an experiment is making sure it is sufficiently focused and precise to test the relevant hypothesis. Every

---

[10] John R. Taylor, An Introduction to Error Analysis: The Study of Uncertainties in Physical Measurements, Second Edition (University Science Books, Sausalito, CA), 1982.

scientist would like to obtain results so compelling that they strongly support or reject the hypothesis. Frequently, however, experimental results are complicated by marginal precision, statistical noise, and systematic phenomena that could not be fully removed or foreseen. In sciences such as astronomy and the biomedical sciences a "better experiment" typically cannot be done. Consequently, probability theory and statistics, like mathematics, are essential tools in scientific research.

In order to calculate the probability of a hypothesis, it is necessary to understand the logic of *conditional probabilities*. It's well understood that if you do a fair flip of a coin, since it has two sides, the probability of it landing with the heads side up is 50%. The more times the coin is flipped, the closer the proportion of heads and tails is to 50% heads and 50% tails. If you flip two coins the probability of getting two heads is 25%, since there are now four possibilities and two heads is only one of those four possibilities. Since the coin flips are independent, we also know we can calculate the probability of two heads by multiplying the probability of getting heads for each coin: 50% of 50% is 25%. What if, however, the probability of getting heads with one of the coins depends on the probability of getting heads with the other coin? In this (admittedly unlikely) case, the assumption of independent coins and this 25% probability are not correct. The probability of getting heads is now conditional on the probability of getting heads with the other coin.

As a demonstration of the power of conditional probabilities, I have chosen the example of a home COVID-19 test. These tests were developed to provide a quick and easy answer to the question

"Do I have COVID-19?" I will test the hypothesis "If I test positive, I have COVID-19." The instructions accompanying the test state that, compared to the molecular SARS-CoV-2 test, the home test correctly identified 83.5% of positive specimens and 99.2% of negative specimens. An equivalent statement is that the test has a 16.5% probability of giving a negative result if you have COVID-19 (a false negative) and a 0.8% chance of giving a positive result if you do not have COVID-19 (a false positive).

To test this hypothesis I need a tool from the theory of conditional probabilities called Bayes' theorem. It is a logical identity attributed to the English Reverend Thomas Bayes (1701 - 1761) and further developed and applied in subsequent centuries. For this test it states the following:

> the probability you have COVID-19 if you test positive is *equal to*
> the probability you will test positive if you have COVID-19 *times* the probability you have COVID-19 before taking the test
> *divided by* the probability of testing positive.

The home test provider has told us the probability of testing positive if you have COVID-19 is 83.5%. Determining the probability you have COVID-19 before taking the test is more difficult. This is typically an estimate of the percentage of people in the region on the day the test is taken who have tested positive for COVID-19. This can depend on whether you are vaccinated or unvaccinated and other individual behaviors. For illustration I will use the average daily cases per 100,000 people in the northeast United States reported by the New York Times.[11] On 2022 January 10 the average daily cases peaked at 302 per 100,000 people. For comparison, on 2023 March 22 six cases per 100,000 people are reported. These relative frequencies correspond to percentages of 0.302% and 0.006%, respectively.

The probability of testing positive is the probability that you test positive *and* have COVID-19, *plus* the probability that you test positive *and do not* have COVID-19. Using the logic of conditional probabilities, this can be restated as the probability you will test positive if you have COVID-19 *times* the probability you have COVID-19 before taking the test, *plus* the probability you will test positive if you *do not* have COVID-19 *times* the probability you *do not* have COVID-19 before you take the test. The probability you will test positive if you do not have COVID-19 is the false positive rate of 0.8%. The prior probability that you do not have COVID-19 is 100% - 0.302% = 99.698% on 2022 January 10, and 100% - 0.006% = 99.994% on 2023 March 22.

We now have all the percentages we need to solve Bayes' theorem for the probability of having COVID-19 if you test positive. At the peak on 2022 January 10, this comes out to be just 24%! Even worse, on 2023 March 22 the probability of having COVID-19 is 0.622%. These numbers do not inspire great confidence in the hypothesis. However, they also do not rule out the possibility that you have COVID-19.

---

[11] https://www.nytimes.com/interactive/2021/us/covid-cases.html

What if, instead of testing positive, you tested negative? Bayes' theorem can be applied again to determine the probability you have COVID-19 if you test negative. On 2022 January 10 this comes out to be 0.05%, as compared to your estimated prior probability of 0.302%. On 2023 March 22 your probability of having COVID-19 is just under 0.001%, as compared to your estimated prior probability of 0.006%. The test does an excellent job of indicating that you do not have COVID-19 if you test negative. The hypothesis that you have COVID-19 if you test negative is found to be unacceptable.

What if you take the home test again after testing positive and you test positive again? The previous positive test updated your knowledge of the probability that you have COVID-19. Now we can use Bayes' theorem again to calculate the probability you have COVID-19 given that you tested positive. This time, however, the probability you have COVID-19 before taking the second test is the probability computed for the first test. Instead of 0.302% and 0.006%, the prior probability of having COVID-19 before taking the second test is 24% on 2022 January 10 and 0.622% on 2023 March 22. Using these prior probabilities, the probability you have COVID-19 on 2022 January 10 is now 96.2% and on 2023 March 22 it's 39.5%.

These somewhat tedious calculations illustrate several important points about this home test. First, the greater the incidence of COVID-19 in your area or, more generally, the greater the chance you may have COVID-19 prior to taking the test, the greater confidence you can have that a positive result means you have COVID-19. Second, you can significantly increase your confidence in the positive test result by taking the test again. When your likelihood of having been exposed to COVID-19 is low, after two positive results you may want to take a third test or, better, avoid contact with other people and contact a doctor about a more accurate test. Third, if you test negative, the probability you have COVID-19 is quite low.

Now, what about scientific hypotheses in general? For an arbitrary scientific hypothesis with data obtained to test the hypothesis, Bayes' theorem can be stated as follows:

> the probability of the hypothesis given the data is *equal to* the probability of the data given the hypothesis *times* the probability of the hypothesis *divided by* the probability of the data.

The probability of the data given the hypothesis is the likelihood that the relevant data, accounting for the uncertainty in the data, would be obtained assuming the hypothesis is correct. This is typically a statistical distribution for the difference between the data and values predicted by the hypothesis, such as the Normal distribution (bell curve), with a width determined by the uncertainty in the data. The greater the difference between the data and the predicted values, the smaller the probability of the data given the hypothesis.

The probability of the hypothesis is typically a statistical distribution containing any prior knowledge about the prediction based on the hypothesis. If there is no prior knowledge, it might be a flat distribution, indicating that all values are equally probable. If the predicted values are known to be confined to a certain range of values, it can contain that information. Fortunately, any incorrect information that might be included in this prior distribution is eventually lost as more tests are performed (new experiments or observations) and the original probability of the hypothesis is replaced by the probability of the hypothesis given the new data. Essentially, any unjustified assumptions that may have been included in the prior probability are tested and, if incorrect, eventually rejected.

The probability of the data, unlike the probability of the data given the hypothesis, is independent of any hypothesis. The COVID-19 example had only two possibilities, either you have COVID-19 or you don't. Therefore, the probability of the data, in that case the probability of testing positive, was the probability of testing positive and you have COVID-19 plus the probability of testing positive and you do not have COVID-19. In general, the probability of the data is summed (or integrated) over all values both the tested hypothesis and all related hypotheses might have predicted. It assures that, given the data, the sum of the probability of all relevant hypotheses is 100%.

Bayes' theorem provides a way to quantitatively compare the probability of two or more hypotheses. For the COVID-19 example we can compare the probability of having COVID-19 if you test positive to the probability of not having COVID-19 if you test positive. Since these are the only two possibilities, the probability of not having COVID-19 if you test positive is simply 100% minus the probability you have COVID-19 if you test positive. A convenient way to compare these two hypotheses is the odds ratio, here the ratio of the probability you have COVID-19 if you test positive to the probability you do not have COVID-19 if you test positive. For the first 2022 January 10 test, this ratio is 0.32. It's a bit more than three times more likely you do not have COVID-19 than you do have it! After the second positive test, however, this odds ratio is about 25, so it is 25 times more likely you do have COVID-19 than you don't! On 2023 March 22 when the incidence of COVID-19 was much lower, a third positive result with the home test is required before the probability of having COVID-19 exceeds the probability of not having it.

Scientists often have a long string of data to fit with a mathematical model. A typical example is the spectrum of light from a star or other astronomical object, consisting of the brightness of light observed at a sequence of wavelengths. The mathematical model is based on a physical model for the shape of the spectrum, but it contains a number of variables that are unknown until the data are fitted with the model. Bayes' theorem can be used to determine the most probable values of these unknown variables as well as the uncertainty in them, based on the data and the uncertainty in the data. This is done by minimizing differences between the data and spectral values predicted by the model, consequently maximizing the probability of the model given the data (and accounting for the uncertainties in the data). This can be a daunting task, especially when the number of unknown variables is large (but smaller than the number of data points).

For simple models, the simplest being a straight line, simpler methods exist for fitting the model to the data. These simpler methods can in fact be derived from Bayes' theorem. In general, however, the uncertainty in any variable of the model is conditional on the uncertainty in the other variables. The computational effort required to compute both the most probable values of these variables and the uncertainty in them can be extensive. Fortunately, the availability of fast computers and efficient algorithms has made this feasible. In particular, Markov chain Monte Carlo (MCMC) algorithms are used to find these most probable values and map out the probability space around them. The probability of the model itself can also be assessed. This is a substantial improvement in our ability to evaluate complex models.

Bayes' theorem provides a formal, mathematical implementation of the Scientific Method. This should not be surprising, since conditional probabilities are intrinsic to the Scientific Method. Every scientific hypothesis, theory, law, or model is conditional on the data obtained to test it. For two models that are both consistent with the available data, if one of them is simpler in that it requires fewer variables to fit the data than the other, Bayes' theorem favors the simpler model. As we saw for the COVID-19 test example, each time a hypothesis (or model) is independently tested, if it is found to be acceptable its probability (given the validity of the data) increases.

There are many books on Bayesian analysis for the mathematically inclined. Several are listed in the footnotes below[12][13][14] and others, including many relevant websites, can be found through an internet search. The use of Bayesian statistical analysis and statistics in general in science has long been controversial. In science statistics is a tool. If statistical analysis becomes the goal rather than a worthwhile tool to test the acceptability of a scientific hypothesis or model, it can become a hindrance to scientific progress. It can also be abused if its application is not well understood. Once understood, the value of conditional probabilities and Bayes' theorem to applications of the Scientific Method is evident.

---

[12] Bolstad, William M., Introduction to Bayesian Statistics, Second Edition (Wiley-Interscience, Hoboken, NJ), 2007.

[13] Silva, D. S. (with J. Skilling), Data Analysis: A Bayesian Tutorial, Second Edition (Oxford University Press, Oxford, UK), 2006.

[14] Gregory, Phil C., Bayesian Logical Data Analysis for the Physical Sciences, A Comparative Approach with Mathematica™ Support (Cambridge University Press, Cambridge, UK), 2005.

Chapter 8
Good Work! Now Do It Again.

The first important step of the Scientific Method is to pay attention to the natural world and ask questions. Nothing will be accomplished without this step. The second important step is to formulate a testable hypothesis (Chapter 2). This focuses your question into a statement that can be shown to be either acceptable or incorrect. Be sure to keep it simple (Chapter 5). Make a prediction based on this hypothesis that you can test with either observations or an experiment. Before carrying out your observations or experiment, do some research to find out what is already known related to your hypothesis (Chapter 3). This survey of the related literature may lead you to revise or change your hypothesis. Once you have settled on a hypothesis, you determine what needs to be tested and can be tested, then plan and carry out your experiment or observations (Chapter 4). Whatever result you obtain (acceptable or incorrect), be sure to report it and clearly explain how you obtained it (Chapter 6).

The purpose of the Scientific Method is to learn by testing hypotheses, not to prove a belief to be true. The test must not be biased by a strongly held belief and both positive and negative results must be acceptable and reported. Neutrality and openness to whatever result is obtained are critical to scientific enquiry. As emphasized in previous chapters, a scientific hypothesis cannot be proven to be true. With repeated testing, however, its validity can be shown to be highly probable, at least under certain conditions (Chapter 7). Hence the need for the process to continue and evolve.

In the past a few scientists have suggested that everything is known in their discipline, there is nothing more to do. In each case they have turned out to be wrong. We have seen that science generally progresses at a slow pace, with decades or more passing between major advances. This is often because of the interplay between scientific advances and technological advances. Support, or lack of it, by society is also a major factor. The scientific process itself of formulating ideas (hypotheses), testing them, disseminating them, and further testing them is always a factor.

Some people are uncomfortable with the idea that scientific hypotheses and, therefore, our understanding of the natural world can never be proven to be absolutely true and, therefore, are probabilistic. It is important to recognize, however, that these probabilities can be very large (close to 100%) or very small (close to 0%), and they are conditional on circumstances and the amount of testing. When the scientific community generally agrees that the probability of a scientific hypothesis is close to 0% (how close depends on the hypothesis), it is considered to be incorrect. If the probability is close to 100%, it becomes a scientific fact.

As a simple numerical example, a scientific fact learned by most students in an elementary physics class is that the acceleration due to gravity at the surface of Earth is 9.8 meters per second per second.

However, if the condition "at the surface of Earth" is changed to the altitude of the International Space Station (about 420 kilometers above Earth's surface), this drops to about 8.7 meters per second per second. Since Earth's surface has a range of altitudes, this value is also somewhat different if for some reason a more precise measurement of the acceleration due to gravity is needed. The value of the number is conditional on where and how it is used. Newton's laws, also conditional scientific facts, explain how and why these numbers are obtained.

The probabilistic nature of scientific hypotheses is reflected in everyday life. If you cross a busy city street there is always some probability you will be hit by a car. This probability is conditional on events you cannot control, such as visibility (if a car can suddenly appear from around a blind corner or run a red light, for example) and the rate at which cars pass by, as well as events you can control, such as where you cross and how carefully you watch the traffic. If you cross the street with your eyes and ears focused on your phone, your probability of being hit is much greater than if you carefully watch and listen for the traffic. If you watch for cars multiple times while crossing the street, you are updating and substantially decreasing the probability of being hit each time you look. Crossing at a designated crosswalk also decreases your probability of being hit in most cases. You can decrease your probability of being run over to a percentage sufficiently small that you feel confident you can safely cross. In general, we control our environments to minimize the chance of injury or death.

When you cross a street it is not likely you are calculating and recalculating the probability of being hit by a car. Likewise, scientists are not typically calculating the probability of hypotheses as they are tested. These calculations are valuable, however, for fitting mathematical models to data and for comparing and evaluating these models. They also provide a way for computers to make decisions in artificial intelligence.

I have intentionally left to the end a discussion of the topic of the relationship between science and religion. There is no scientific hypothesis that can be tested to determine whether a god or gods exist. This is purely a matter of faith, which plays no role in the Scientific Method. We have seen that in centuries past some religious leaders have obtained important results in science, mathematics, and probability theory. An interest in religion was accompanied by an interest in obtaining a better understanding of the natural world. Those privileged to obtain a higher education often studied religious texts and the science and mathematics of the time. This broad education became prohibitive as the amount of information exploded and education became more specialized.

I have heard it argued that science and religion are completely separate subjects and have no impact on each other. This is incorrect. Religious beliefs are testable when they make a clear statement about the intervention of a supreme being (or, alternatively, aliens from another planet) in the natural world. One of the best known examples of this was the religious belief that God placed man and Earth at the center of the universe with the known planets orbiting Earth in perfectly circular orbits. Astronomical observations and the Scientific Method ultimately made it impossible for a rational human being to accept this premise (Chapter 5). Some (but not all) religious leaders made life quite difficult for the scientists who promoted this new knowledge. Change is often particularly difficult for and resisted by those who fear a loss of power over other people.

Another major example is the conclusion that Earth and humankind were created on 22 October 4004 BC, based on a careful interpretation of the Bible by James Ussher, Church of Ireland Anglican Archbishop of Armagh in the 17th century. Subsequent Biblical studies have led to the conclusion that The Creation occurred between 6,000 and 10,000 years ago. Science, on the other hand, indicates that Earth formed 4.5 billion years ago and human beings (homo sapiens) emerged around 300,000 years ago. The belief that Earth and life were created less than 10,000 years ago persists, despite substantial scientific evidence to the contrary. This belief today is described as young Earth creationism, scientific creationism, or creation science. It is supported by attempts to reinterpret or discredit the scientific results. There is nothing scientific about scientific creationism, however. Contrary to the Scientific Method, its supporters attempt to prove a belief rather than test hypotheses. No new, reproducible scientific evidence is provided. Despite its name, creation science does not employ the Scientific Method and, therefore, is not science.

A belief not based on religion that is almost as old as humankind is astrology, the belief that the relative positions of the Sun, planets and stars in the sky can be used to predict human characteristics and affairs. Numerous scientific tests have been applied to various aspects of astrology (not to be confused with the scientific field, astronomy). None have provided evidence in support of astrology having any predictive capabilities.[15]

    I became a scientist for the joy of learning about the natural world and how it works, and the opportunity to contribute to this knowledge. Also significant draws were working with the latest technology, some of it quite impressive in both capabilities and size, and the opportunity to travel around much of the world. Science in itself is neither good nor bad. What matters is how scientific knowledge is used. It is always an advantage to have a better, deeper understanding of ourselves and our world. However, that knowledge can be used for destructive purposes. It is ultimately up to society to determine how it is used. The Scientific Method ensures that our knowledge of the natural world is accurate. The importance of science is enshrined in the Constitution of the United States in Section 8 of Article I, where it states that Congress shall have power to *promote the progress of science and "useful arts"*.

    The last step of the Scientific Method, after evaluating and recording your result, is to return to the first step and repeat. If the result is positive, in other words you find your hypothesis to be acceptable, a repeated test with essentially the same prediction and experiment would best be done by another scientist or group of scientists. Alternatively, a different prediction or refined hypothesis may be tested. Testing a refined hypothesis can provide new

---

[15]Astrology and science, Wikipedia (https://en.wikipedia.org/wiki/Astrology_and_science)

The Scientific Method

information while indirectly retesting the original hypothesis. If the result is negative, you find your hypothesis to be incorrect, this information can be used to formulate a new, different hypothesis to test. Either way, progress is made in advancing scientific knowledge.

The best way to finish this book is to review the summary of the Scientific Method. With this in mind, I have duplicated The Scientific Method in a Nutshell on the next page. You might want to copy or print it for future reference! If you are a scientist, I hope you found enough new and interesting discussion here to make the read worthwhile. If you are not a scientist, I hope this book has given you a better perspective for understanding and evaluating reports of new scientific results. If you are a teacher, I hope you are inspired to use this perspective to explicitly teach the Scientific Method to your students.

The Scientific Method encourages asking and seeking answers to questions. It encompasses observations, rational thinking, experimentation, and persistence. It is at the core of science, technology, engineering, and mathematics (STEM). It should be explicitly taught to all primary school, secondary school and college students.

Bon voyage!

The Scientific Method in a Nutshell

Ask questions! Follow the steps below to seek an answer to one of these questions.

1. Start with a statement (**hypothesis**) to be tested that is based on your question.

    A valid scientific hypothesis

- **cannot** be proven to be absolutely true
- **can** possibly be shown to be incorrect.

2. Make a **prediction** based on the hypothesis.

3. Search for any information already available pertaining to the validity of the hypothesis and prediction.

4. Make **observations** or devise an **experiment** to test the prediction. Examine the results of the observations or experiment. The results should be

one thing if the hypothesis is acceptable, and something else if it is incorrect.

A hypothesis is acceptable and useful as long as it has not been demonstrated to be incorrect.

5. Revise or change the hypothesis if required by the results. When multiple valid hypotheses can be envisioned, **always choose the simplest hypothesis**.

6. Make methods and results public for comments and future studies. (If you are a professional scientist, **publish** in an appropriate refereed journal and present at scientific society meetings.)

7. **Repeat** with a new experiment or observations to test a refined or revised hypothesis.

About The Author
Gordon Holman

Dr. Gordon Holman is a research scientist who specializes in astrophysics. He earned a Bachelor of Science degree in physics from Florida State University and a Doctor of Philosophy degree in astrophysics from the University of North Carolina at Chapel Hill, where he also assisted with and taught undergraduate courses in astronomy and physics. In his Ph. D. thesis he developed models for the X-ray and radio emissions observed from between the galaxies in large clusters of galaxies. After receiving his Ph. D., he taught courses and conducted research at the University of Maryland in College Park. For most of his career he was a research astrophysicist at the National Aeronautics and Space Administration's (NASA's) Goddard Space Flight Center in Greenbelt, Maryland. His primary scientific focus at Goddard Space Flight Center was on obtaining a better understanding of solar flares using data obtained from space- and ground-based observatories. He was a Co-Investigator for NASA's Reuven Ramaty High Energy Solar Spectroscopic Imager (RHESSI), an Earth-orbiting satellite that observed the Sun in high-energy X rays and gamma rays. He retired from NASA in 2018.

Printed in Great Britain
by Amazon